BY JOAN METELERKAMP

Towing the Line (1992)
Stone No More (1995)
Into the Day Breaking (2000)
Floating Islands (2001)
Requiem (2003)
Carrying the Fire (2005)

Burnt Offering

Burnt Offering

Joan Metelerkamp

Versions of some of these poems have appeared in *PEN News, New Coin, New Contrast, Southern Rain Poetry,* and *Litnet.*

The quote on page 29, is reprinted by permission of Open Court Publishing Company, a division of Carus Publishing Company, Peru, IL, from *Anatomy of the Psyche,* copyright © 1994 by Edward F. Edinger.

First published in 2009 by Modjaji Books CC
P O Box 385, Athlone, 7760, South Africa
modjaji.books@gmail.com
http://modjaji.book.co.za

ISBN 978-0-9802729-4-9

Editing: Robert Berold
Text and cover design: Natascha Mostert
Lettering: Hannah Morris
Cover art: Colleen Crawford Cousins

Printed and bound by Harbec Packaging, Cape Town
Set in Palatino 10/13 pt

Cape Tercentenary Foundation

For Frances and Paul

Contents

Prologue

All so still after the rain washed so clear I could cry –
what's to do – check the email for word from her –

what were the long years of narrative like a century
gone, broken, a wall down, *Goodbye Lenin* –

decades of my mother's weekly letters –
this morning so still even if my daughter hadn't left home I could cry.

At last you've broken your obsession with narrative
he said, though the note in the post

said the opposite: I'm still trapped in symbol and analysis
she said, meaning herself, as he did, as he meant himself,

only he couldn't see it, couldn't say it, unless
he saw it in me: who did he see did he see

three coins pressed to my palm under my pen
for calling old symbols again, old analyses – what do I do –

he saw what he was doing, looking at me, reading my poem
breaking open narrative

like a symbol, the host, take, break, like the day
that's what to do –

Points on poems

1. You can begin at any point.

2. You might be asked to account for yourself
   (you are always asking yourself to account for yourself);
   you could start with the point that poems don't sell
   take stock of that fact
   prevaricate, equivocate,

3. leave it as a starting point, for later, balance
   interest, currency, the market;

4. you could come back to it before you had begun you could cycle round
   lugubriously, alternatively

5. get on your bike and ride like hell like we used to, my brothers and I,
   when we were kids –
   careening round the concave concrete cow-shed yard –
   no brakes, no gears –
   sweaty and queasy and
   sometimes skidding on bull-shit.

6. Go, go with its elliptical spin, which is also weirdly comforting because

7. a poem has no point.

8. You could begin again: there is not one point to a poem
   it is always
   another point of departure.

9. Try another point of departure,
   say: poems are like music, not music, but like – the lines
   climax, silence, sound
   their own melodies, yes, but visions
   a score of complex
   moments in process emotion almost beyond words most of all
   what you can hardly, hardly, say, hardly, hardly bear to see, see and then

10. revision. Re-vision, if you must.

11. (Now you see it now you don't).

12. Okay, okay *no ideas but in things* the thing is

13. always the poem:

14. not a record –
    a resonance.

15. But at what point do I come in, you could say,
    and I could say
    either through your eye, through your ear,
    or – what my mother used to say (to thin air)
    when someone in another car hadn't thanked her for letting them in –

16. "not at all".
    Either you get it or you don't.

17. You could ask who speaks when the speaker is I.

18. The point is whose voice, out of the blue, into thin air,
    uses "I", like a child shrieking "me me me",
    or otherwise playing quietly outside under the pines
    whispering "you" "he" "she"?

19. Yours. Mine.

20. The point is: a poem is not a confession,
    it's not a profession (you could go back to the starting point)
    why you do it – it's a puzzle –

21. you could start at the edges
        or go for the gold in the middle –
        the bits where you can't tell
    the reflection from the craft
    floating on the surface, a coracle,
    and the more you piece together
    the figure – like the Lady of Shallot

drifting through the reeds alone –
the more she looks like your daughter
or you, when you were younger,
only where is the river running you begin to wonder
and anyway
there's always a bit missing
and we all know it doesn't really help –
the picture, on the box –

22. you're always figuring out
    what isn't fixed even if you think it is: or
    it is
    but still, and precisely still –

23. even though my brother, when we were older
    (though, according to the song, I'm so much younger than that now)
    and I was already a mother,
    used to say: don't fix it unless it's broken.

24. This is an old story
        like Keats's figures on the jar,
    still chasing
    what they want, what they want to become,
    happy, happy –

    but everything empty, the vessel, the town –
    they'll never be more than they are.

25. A poem isn't a record nor is it a performance. But like
    live drawing the essential figure moving,
    how do you get it moving

26. across the page?
    (There should be no limit to the number of pages.)

27. It has nothing to do with linear narrative
    even though it's made of lines,
    and although it is really a story,

28. where to begin? What is the point
    of entry?

29. The song of the fertility doll (phallic and female)
    the energy that's divine
    (golden girl playing the piano
    easy, jazzy, smiling, explaining
    her hands are two Russian dolls
    they do exactly what she tells them to).

30. What on earth am I talking about - *cling, cohere, persevere?*

31. Don't ask unless you think it's somehow answerable or unavoidable,

32. like voices.

33. St Joan believed even when she couldn't hear the voices any longer

34. to the point of burning alive.

35. What do the voices say?
    What do you feel?
    Can you make them come

36. like someone else's voice? Another poet's?
    These poems are usually the best.
    As though someone else's words came into your head when you wake
    like after the recurring dream of intruders,
    you're sweating that fear of death sweat   you've spent all this time
    worrying at that point   you know
    Eliot made sixty years ago "the still point of the turning world"

37. and he was only re-writing the ancients and

38. who gives you the right to write what you like
    any way, who's to say if it makes any sense,
    any one – anyway –
    all poems are illegitimate.

39. Get used to this. You can't do anything else.
    Language itself is the transgressor.
    We know this. This is as old as Prometheus.
    "Yes, but what does this mean?"
    Nothing to do with what those who know better call
    "your personal life".

40. Who do you think you're talking to in that tone of voice
    like "get a life"?

41. You, me; myself – a poet is always talking to herself –
    even more than to the dead. Answering back.

42. If the poem makes its own meaning, makes it up as it goes along,
    (I could come back to this) is something (what thing –
     the thing the poem is) prior to the poem –
    need the question arise?

43. It does
    arise
    like a god rises
    you can't not
    feel this
    how to say what it was, is,
    when it's just light you know
    through the slit through the curtains
    white light of the night
    turning to day
    like a lover turning over
    through that opening, that parting,
    that deep coming leaving
    only your need
    to speak –
    ignore this, silence it,
    what will come into becoming?

44. Then instead of moving
     (in bewilderment, perhaps, not knowing where to ask
     for the words for this)
     like through the cool passages of an imagined labyrinth
     (but sometimes it's hot like hot is cool
     or sick is really cool
     like kids down a slippery slide)
     instead, you get your head tangled, line after line
     like a spider in a spider's web:
     Arachne, still weaving the stuff out of herself,
     battered over the head with her own distaff
     by the jealous goddess;
     rather be Ariadne,
     lending her golden thread
     to her hero, to find his way out of the labyrinth,
     yes, he abandons her, but who finds her in the end:
     the one who comes back: Dionysus.

45. What labyrinth? The question is
     where the hell is this
     'waar's ons nou' (as they say on the phone
     in Karatara)?
     When the crystals are dislodged
     the diamond body falls,
     you feel as though you might fall over yourself
     every time you reach upwards,
     even if it's to hang out the washing.
     If you think I'm talking about the inner ear I am.

46. If you are too sentimental or conventional for your crystals
     ever to be knocked out of place
     the poems you prefer will be sentimental and conventional –
     probably in tight little rooms
     (room = stanza, in Italian, no doubt someone will explain)
     with a witty bit left hanging which could be anyone's
     do not disturb sign

(you never know what's going on in there)
[of course there are little rooms where when
is a jar not a jar but a door left just off its jamb
opening something we didn't know we could imagine].

47. If you lose your balance completely no one will want to follow there.

48. "Sixth and lastly" – as the dogsbody policeman says –
    Much Ado about Nothing –
    the main point about poetry

49. you don't find it in airports or bookclubs,
    and if Nadine Gordimer were to ask you
    if she could publish your work
    for some cause, like AIDS, or even with no cause
    with no payment to you at all you'd say, here, have it *all*,
    please.

50. Cold comfort: the so-called
    helpers at the bookshop in Plettenberg Bay
    have never heard of Nadine Gordimer.
    So how do you make a living, poet, I ask myself,
    not for nothing

51. there are more ways of silencing a poet than with a Sentence.

52. This has nothing to do with The People's Poet.

53. This has nothing to do with The Woman Poet.

54. (The point is, nice girls always lie –
    to protect the innocent –
    there is a point beyond which
    they do not think;
    think what their good friends
    might think.)
    (Go directly to that point – do not collect R200).

55. If it's only amusement play, play,
    taking yourself seriously, amusing yourself, seriously,
    see what keeps
    coming up
    like say you keep coming up with an old symbol,
    the Dionysian heart in a basket,
    how do you say it –

56. the heart's thought, what does it mean, the eternal return,
    like the baby's heart on the monitor
    your own arrhythmia
    heart in your head on the bed –

    Not the apotheosis but the pattern the poet said.

57. But the pattern always appears
    when you're doing something else
    following some other thread
    you aren't listening or looking
    you're driving towards
    something else,
    like driving in the heat of the day up Keyter's Nek
    to fetch your teenage son after school
    head cruising any way
    into the road's rhythm, the heat,
    windows wide, words gone any way
    like *affirmation of the affirmation,*
    and you know this has very little to do with "positive thinking"
    in fact you're beginning to think it's the opposite,
    the words return, and there's no way to pull off the road,
    pull out of its rhythm to look, listen,
    to make them some pattern
    some sound to hear clearly not like like, like love, like love,
    not like this, this,
    but I've lost it again like this –
    not some thing like love not like any thing but this.

58. Or you wake in the night to the hot still after a storm,
      one of the two black south-eastern warning storms of the season,
      mud smell of water receding,
      frogs down below in the vlei,
      listen,
      an old propeller, an old engine, an old crock car,
      and you don't mind any more where you're spinning in any old world
      nor that the song the frogs make
      makes no more sense than this –
      the ballad the wind sings through the reeds
      through the house on a hot afternoon, sad,
      repetitive, like to a baby in the bulrushes (the heart in a basket)
      the scales you can hear clearly
      of what the poet calls *marvelous*

      out of sight out of mind
      below surface,
      (like a mole-rat shaking and shaking the roots of a khakibos
      and all you can see is the thin plant shaking: okay, take it, it's just a weed).

59. Below surface, the words of the dead,
      dreams, too.
      I'll make one point: a poet can't live in daylight too long:
      the chainsaw in the valley;
      the chainsong of canaries, cisticolas, sombre bulbul, sunbirds,
      despite the cloud cover;
      the script of named fynbos; the clear horizon, the still sea;
      the discomfort of day's plans, narratives, narratives.

60. Wake to a snippet of dream recalled:
      I am off to get my own handcuffs, my own truncheon,
      hurry up they're waiting for me
      on the other side of the street like opposite the parking lot
      they blew up in Pretoria
      and I am young again as I was then when I lived in Pretoria.

61. Not what he *said* in the dream,
    what he *felt*, felt what I
    felt, I was dreaming, I felt his coming in,
    I think he said something,
    I felt I was coming in like through a door
    through my body
    I felt his cock I took it held it to my breathing
    I am alive so loudly I am grunting in, I am
    aware even in the dream of my breathing
    his speaking saying
    take it
         take it in.

62. I suppose I may have invented him; I may have been given him:
    I didn't choose the metaphor, it chose me, came to me;
    like a voice, like given words,
    a message, open at this passage:
    the activity of perception or sensation in Greek is aesthesis which means at root
    'taking in' and 'breathing in' – a 'gasp', that primary aesthetic response.

63. Only it didn't feel like a message, but a man.
    Like a poem. Not like love but love.

64. There is only one point – begin again – make a poem of it –

Penelope

If I were a woman working
        a myth I could make my own –

making, unmaking,
        all that stuff
        repeating
        whatever you read about a woman writing
what does it matter
                        I could simply say undoing
                                unravelling
        unconscious –

(this sun: leaching all the energy out of me
and head aching, sun: I need shape, form, I need dream, sun,
I need help).

A book, like the bookclub ladies' books
Joan, why don't you write a book?

If I were a woman working
                who could answer

why do you think Penelope pulled out all that knitting
every evening
creeping, unheard, unweaving

every morning
back to the first line –

do we even know what she was making?

        The pure necessity – a shroud
                for the old king

what was it, king,
what was the image ingrained,
what was the feel, the form,
the ecphrasis,

the work of art, in other words, within the work of art?

Imagine it, what was it was woven,
woven together as unanswerable riddles?

The train went over the bridge
What was the driver's name?

Driven by the question

Penelope all day at it all night
with her handmaid
pulling it all out
like a nightmare, a dream anyway, where you never get anywhere

only eventually
over twenty two years…

Perhaps, my daughter suggests (perhaps she only imagines it),
what she was weaving, Penelope: the story of Odysseus –
to bring him back –
her own story in other words
to make the masculine more secure

couldn't she weave
to save her life
to save his life
she took it all out again –

you've written yourself
and written yourself off
a long time –

head still aching its head off:
burnt out like the modem blitzed by lightning
(like a fool I left it plugged in)

✦

Head stuck in the fence, will utterly undirected
afraid of the hard and strong
unable to turn this way or that
since Sunday –

sheep with its head in the fence
or rooikat
after you'd eaten forty lambs and my brother finally caught you
and caged you – bleeding
above your right eye
(taken you off to the Tsitsikamma and don't be a bloody fool
and come back).

Shall I pull it all out, my knitting, I thought –
I woke this morning thinking of knitting: like a picket fence
needles pulled out
fence of rib with the loops all loose –
imagine walking around with that on your back, wrote Anne Sexton –
imagine walking around with a picket fence
(only I didn't see it – my head's been stuck in it since Sunday)
Anne Sexton's letters I've been stuck in them since Sunday
acting upon me *like a misfortune*
serving *as an axe*
leaking all over the page bleeding to hell and gone –

I dreamt a little blue car
"whose car is that" I woke thinking, forgetting
my own
"bloo jool" I thought "it's Anne Sexton's"

but it was trapped under a timber truck
could anyone have got out alive
no no no no no
      it is impossible!
           get out of there alive!

there is a long thin fury
      whacking a plank
           fallen from the truck

get out of there!
      she strikes the truck –
           hits back –

✦

I can tell you
it wasn't my weaving that saved me –
if you can call this saved
sometimes I think I'm finished with that –
will I go back,
is it finished or not?
All that doubt, all that sweat
with the fucking suitors –

it was my son, it was Telemachus, obviously,

going off to parties, yes, and singing in rock concerts
and all the girls all round him and always
on the phone to his friends who haven't listened in class
and preparing
for his last tests
and nervous
and tired
of being the only responsible one and president of the SRC –

but I'm his mother after all
and I can tell you something
(as I told my friend and she said:
"isn't that *dependence*"
but actually this is my odyssey)

when I look at him I see
            he needs me
not fussing obsessing counting and keeping

calm down, mother, take it easy –

what he needs
            is my faith
as the fates say
that's all, really, he needs nothing of me.

✦

When the old king lies in his sick bed
waking from a dream cries
'you are free, free – let your son
go off and become an artisan'

I dismiss my first thought –
is this your way of dissing my son
your refusal to see he's a prince – your grandson –

instead I thank him –
he's saying: you are living as you choose –

but the weight of his words, like
make something
of all the old responsibility picked up and carried
since my last year at school
of those to whom much is given much will be required

earlier, thirteen when I learnt the words
for the part I had by heart
o my father, had I the tongue of Orpheus
to make the stones to leap and follow me....
do not take away this life of mine
before its dying time –

take myself to bed with my ten day aching head
and vertigo, let the world spin;
and as I lie there watching the wind as I lie there –
nothing –
who sees the wind after all?

All this energy all this endless spinster-like activity
trying to keep myself together – for what –
for nothing, for breaking with pain spinning
          out of control
there was nothing else for it.

26

When he gets back he lies like Odysseus
on my bed in my workroom and cries –
he doesn't even know which lines have moved him
he doesn't really know why; he knows why
I've been working
he is so exhausted – all of it – we had to do it –

✦

Penelope: perhaps like the wicked queen
she wasn't on the right side of those little impulses,
the ones who would have finished her work for her –
or even like the young queen
wanting to keep her king and her baby
if she weren't obsessively looking at herself in the mirror splitting
hairs, splitting
apart every night;
if she could just have let it be
sleeping, dreaming

if she weren't wanting to make it all the time
if she weren't worrying about her husband
this weaving of heroes and heroic dissent and descent and constant
contest and success –
or even if she weren't so determined every day
as if she were going out to find food while he wandered!
to fish, say, for her family

cast on cast off, drop, pick up, carry,

if she just allowed a little more slack if she afforded a little more give
if she let the lines rest a little, released, delivered like *I fish in your give.*

Alchemical Incantations

The central image of alchemy is the idea of the *opus*. The alchemist thought of himself as committed to a sacred work – a search for the supreme and ultimate value.... After the *prima materia* has been found, it has to submit to a series of chemical procedures in order to be transformed.... There is no exact number of alchemical operations, and many images overlap.... They are *calcinatio, solutio, coagulatio, sublimatio, mortifactio, separatio, and coniunctio*. (... Latin terms instead of calcination, solution, and so on, in order to distinguish the psychological processes from the chemical procedures).

- *Edward Edinger "Anatomy of the Psyche"*

Burning

I burnt my book – I burnt
blocks of it, like brittle briquettes,
long after I imagined burning it –
I imagined the backs curl back in flames
covering the cover, carrying the fire –
I imagined
I couldn't do it:
I would fling my body across my books like I imagined
flinging my body
across my mother's to bring her back –
listen,
  it was just an accident
  just a moment of madness
like a marriage going up in flames after a fight –

  (but my son
  standing at the kitchen counter crying
I don't know how
I couldn't have seen it:
but my son:
but I didn't)

    ✦

friable February has fallen –
out of this window look out at the dune
lying like a burnt dog – its back like a dog with mange –
lying low licking its wounds

slow salamander
we saw you get up and shake yourself free
I stood in the dark on the stoep with my son

we saw you alight, flames thirty foot flaring
mane of the gums shaking and flaming
stick figure men shouting
back burning the break –

✦

dune lying down resigned
burnt back to the burning sun
as long as I live
you will live –
as long as my children's children live
and who knows if they will know you –

Burnt offering

Like old accusations – sweep them away –
burn them –
fireplace like a waste paper basket, papers piled on
old ash
old thoughts, unfinished stories, letters, journals –
sore throats, blocked ears, headaches,
listlessness –

how many years it takes how many lists
it takes them all –

through grievance past grief
              back to ground
              solid enough

here where we've built our house
close to the sea, overlooking the river, the valley,

poppies in the wind now and earlier in the season watsonias
filling the hill behind the camphor bush filling the air
and next year, who knows, maybe the porcupine will have got them
like he got my father's lilies –

✦

I dreamt the dream I called Lily Joseph is Dead.
Who the hell is Lily Joseph asked the homeopath
when I told her we could hardly stop laughing
like you laugh like when you're kids
like my son and his friend, Jessie and Paul, laughing, sixteen and
seventeen
and how long
          will love last
forever

who is Lily Joseph I asked the librarian
(when they told me she was dead)
my mother and the librarian looking at me
as if to say: really! Didn't I know!
the poet laureate, she said;

consciously, who is Lily Joseph, I asked myself, really:
the woman-who-does-the-right-thing – like Helen Joseph – in history –
St. Joseph's Lily
(not the real-wife Mary who fucked it up with the angel, literally)
Lily, Lily Briscoe, the artist, at the start of the story –
Lily, like Laurel, the one who wins the laurels –

Lily Joseph is dead was the name of the dream
like *Morrison* was the name of the poet in the story I started to write
like *How – I didn't know any word for it – how "unlikely"*
like simply to be

✦

I dreamt of Lesego;
I dreamt of that poet
with all the burning you could ever dream of
all hell let loose –
who could imagine it
let alone live it;
he wouldn't have come if it weren't a crisis –
he'd lost his bravura, his beret,
he came only with tenderness –

how to make something of this
how not to doubt or not only to doubt
how not to be the old woman sleepless
at the start of the work
unable to write –

that story I was beginning, writing,
opening with the poet untying
the knot, letting the line loose
for the little boat to cross –

✦

After "Lily Joseph" I knew I would never write that story –
even for Morrison, my protagonist, my burning poet, my grieving poet,
to keep him from counting the syllables,
        counting the days,
to keep him from burning his mattress, burning his skin, burning his poems

when I think of you in your ashes, burnt,
like who knows how many countless, uncountable,
unaccountable, unaccounted for,
incinerated
who might never have been –
take this day, here, take it
all its clarity, all its gold –

Dissolving in its own water

jump in the lake I say
in my dream
to that problem solving poet,
that acceptable, allegorical poet,
the one whose bag of hockey sticks I have to carry,
the one who said she didn't like my work, at all, really,
jump in the bloody lake lady –

I'd been kissing a shrivelled poet,
dark, dishevelled, kissing his hair, his forehead,
but that was before his shrinking started,
that was when he was still on a call to his broker
hug me I asked him kissing him slumping
onto the pavement
hitting the gutter

goodbye goodbye you know I love you
I am waving at my own grown children

and they are completely cool and so am I
and only after goodbye
this longing for the once tall man who once had a cell phone
broken now and in the gutter

ink in puddles pooling on the paper
like long ago in the jotter
Eilleen Nicholas weeping water marks all over her crayola
crying for my silent brother next to her failure

Mrs. Beukes with the soap and water –
what could she have said –
what the hell – bloody
bloody hell –
washing her mouth out –

✦

sit in the chair and cry
sit down to write –
the words seep, leak
like the bad breath of a shrunken man
wrapped against the weather –

✦

do dreams only come at the last moment
as if, if they came any sooner, you might collapse –

you are collapsing, and something, something reminds you –

wake to your head splitting, bleeding over the bedclothes,
remembering skinning your face where you collapse against the fence

(the publisher who promised to distribute your books laughing
with the one who urged you not to publish in the first place)

the woman pressed against the fence turning
into someone else, calling

curious horses and cows
curious comfort of their faces pressing
moist breathing –

✦

how could I dream
it could have been a solution

moon gold in the vlei
        risen
silver in the river
        as if this were a solution

Sea

To have lost even the why or the what for –
to dream and to wake with the weight
of even the mechanical why even the mechanical wherefore –

the primitive one-string cello,
bent low playing a threnody, thread, theme I know,
into the night as I wake heaving it, hearing it –

like a chorus dissolving
not only sadness, sea,
                 but past sadness
past past sadness

now that I live so close to your sound, sea,
          even at night wake to listen for you –
          close to your smell
          close and often to your salvage
          your changing sand and rock shelf, sea,
                    lost generations
                    lost progenitors
                    past sadness, sea

Down to earth

for Richard Murphy

In a dream the daughter of two poets,
Emily, a woman of fifty (like me)
begins to cry she looks away and up at the sky
she says: it was like this: her mother said goodbye
so as not to tell the children –

in fact her mother did suicide
using drugs and alcohol to do it
mine did too (like Emily's mother did)
like her own mother did
with a gun no goodbye –

what don't we tell the children –
what can't we call up can't we name
what they don't know   we don't know
they go to the same school, after all, Theo and Paul –
(as their grandmothers, the same school, another school)

I was trying to write a poem for Theodora –
I thought it was a novel, really, but that's another story –
(something to do with my daughter's aliveness my daughter's radiance
her second name her grandmother's
second name, Alice, sweet alyssum, wild alyssum)

for the love of god, Theodora,
for her grandmother's posthumous novel
(the one she wrote when she thought
she was no longer a poet –
the one she couldn't get published –)

Theo: hair loose, eyes loose, openly
bored, slumped in your grandfather's couch
in your skimpy vest and spring limbs
while Paul stood at the foot of the books
paying obeisance:

your grandfather: the poet: saying
"it seems, Theodora, he likes them", but you, quick:
"that's because he's such a liar, Rick" –

in the dream the poets' daughter
Theo's mother – Emily – comes to me –
as she came to me at Fruit & Veg City
saying she hoped our kids would keep friendly –

simply, unabashed, after her cry, she is ready:
we are falling at high speed
down a lift shaft
crawling from the cage
as we hit the basement.

Incarnate

for Robert

After my friend the poet came back
after he'd been away for more than a year
after a night
and then at last a walk on the beach

the invisible current –
     what had he said? he'd said
        it's all finished –
        his carrying that connection between poets –
it's just that other conversation now, I said,
like in that *Conversation in Moscow*, it's only for god,
(he said he wanted to get back to that –
     I thought he'd always been at it)

         though god! god, if I knew what that meant
         would I need to write it at all, let alone
               to it, for it – work at it –
        if I knew what it was
          what it were
          could be is –
        if I knew what I am, who, could be, let alone god –

        conversation with god
what it is in a poem if not conversation with another
part of yourself, perhaps, belligerent, argumentative,
me and you and all the anonymous yous and all the old poets
talking to me, whom they've never heard of, let alone imagined –

after he'd gone –

not that I'm using poems any more, I said,
not that they're using me –
not that I carry any more burning, like sex, say,
        hunger, eating, or bathing, say, or sleep –

the vehicle you're making, my husband said, and the way
the wheel travels to whatever it is you're driving at –

that night I dreamt two goshawks
one with two huge balls but green
green as a green pigeon
and as I opened the door of the kombi to let them free
a shower from the light then water gushing from the roof
flooding my bag with my papers the one I call my poet's bag –
I suppose the ink was all washed away
the car ruined, the roof collapsed, everything drenched anyway –

in the morning east wind ripping
        in the sun, in detachment, noting
like opening, a stratagem, a strange present,

I suppose the ink would all be washed away
what did my friend the poet say

perhaps it is finished, then
maybe it can really begin

Rock

for Andy Saggerson

After *what for* – how can it be answered –
how:
not *what for* nor *who for* any more –
leave them, who
can answer them –
how:

how peel away the thick husk of the voice
the thick skin of the fifty year old
sinews of someone else's values
bark surrounding the core:

with the skill of kids on the stage
newly learnt instruments spilling
fire and water –
Jessie and Paul –

Rock   me-like-a-hurricane
my son riding the dragon leaping
the steel column of the mike
the dark-eyed river of

smoke
on the water
fire in the sky-I

The hill

I have lived here long enough on this hill
to believe it after all
I'm almost fifty
dune river valley sky sea

what do you mean: believe
I mean: really: this material: this work, this existence
I've always believed actually

just for a while couldn't see the metaphor
for what was the matter
for my mother shot herself like her mother shot herself and I fell
(like I couldn't see my arse for my elbow)
in love with someone else

to tell myself
as I told my brother

and the first thing he said
as we stood on the track on the hill
between the graveyard and the compost heap:

god must have wanted it

Where are you

Schubert lieder – the moon up and the dogs
barking at who knows what
porcupine, skunk, rooikat – not so likely
(but midnight and off after a growl
        so strange so quick
        we are up and whispering in the passage)

moon up, dogs whistling their keen squeaking –
what seemed so urgent –
up, and off into the night –

what seemed so urgent
where are you
        somewhere in Schubert lieder
(I am thinking of the man my husband
never dreamt he'd want to meet, he dreams
he meets, two nights later, he dreams of his books
        two nights after our conversation)

where are you, like a dream, and like Lesego
(whom I dreamt of loose and tender)
somewhere in German, in Schubert lieder –

Bury the dead

"Who is Sylvia?" asks my son –
he tells me to watch the movie –
        Gwyneth Paltrow leans out of the window
        to the guy playing Al Alvarez:
        I feel as though God is speaking through me

        I want to be Al, I want to be more than Al,
        lean into this nervousness
        okay, okay, it's what It means, Sylvia,
                It speaks through all of us –

at the crucial moment my father phones –
                gets through to my cell –
        who's that knocking on the door, who wants to come in?
        okay, okay, I tell him – it's just a movie –
        I know what's left
                the unfinished story

                        ✦

Is there no coming through
and who and what to get through to

black angus, like black bushes in the valley,
black cuckoo *I'm so si-ick*
grey sky
soundless sea

                        ✦

My own books standing in piles breaking nothing
not even their own plastic wrapping
the prison of my own making

kill the poet the poem reads, over the screen,
kill the white woman and so on

Henceforth, From the Mind —
For your whole joy, must spring
                                    I could go on copying
It is all according to the imagination

here in the unknowing, in the heart, alone, and in the mind —

sometimes I fancy I could tell a story
might drag me out of here
(might bring me some companion)
like a story a child tells herself
"and then I was, and then we were"
but always come back to
what comes from what I can hardly say what

            being a poet
                        could have given them

mortification followed by putrefaction

one could bury a dead body of work
let it rot like Uncle Dick's books on the stoep,
like Oupa George's letters, rained on, rotten,

let it stink like the dead mule in the Karatara pass —
for weeks in the pass on the way to school the stench of mule —
not only that the books stand in piles in the house
like shit on the doorstep
but that I should tear down *The Host* from the wall.

Stick it up again —
stand in the sun, in the window —
whiff of dug up mole rat —
peripheral vision
            rock pigeon
pecking dried out dog's vomit —

stand and read
            to partake of the host
                        laid for them and for me

Sorting it out

to be reduced to this –
who can afford this, this opus of such selfishness –
the only way for a poet
you could do something else

what you can make and how little difference you make or
what you can make and how little difference you make –

they're shouting too loud to hear you anyway and it's all
so long ago and always all about money all over again and you're shouting
how to sort it all out
how to make the ends meet
how to make yourself heard
        to hear yourself
        go through it
        all over again:

don't even tell me when there's an advert for a job in the action ads
I don't want to know it: it's like a bloody argument
        doctrinal, dogmatic
        god is sick of it

Marry Maree

I dream: my adopted daughter wants to run off and get married

I'm making up this song as I go along
you can't go off and marry, Maree,
if your own mother won't own you

I'm calling you
Maree! Maree!
I'm telling you you're telling me

I'm telling you
what I told myself clearly
you can't go off and do this really

you can't begin with a small coniunctio
it will end in mortificatio

Marry, Maree,
it's poetry,
it's what they used to call chemistry –
    alchemy –

Come together

I consult the old oracle,
I draw the Dao of Perseverance –
make it all come together –

all, you know, meaning
married to metaphor,
the alchemical conjunction;

the institution of marriage
the enduring union
soft and compliant inside

like hands held
under the bedclothes

you're in a good mood my husband laughs
and I laugh inside, yes, well, wouldn't you be
if you'd played polished keys,
modern music, to well over
however long it lasts –

there he goes into the world with our whistling son –
I lie back, glance at recipe books, consider supper,
consider a party when our daughter comes back,
consider the lilies,
consider the spring, decide it's begun
get up: bring it all together:
get into that matter.

Intact

we are back
to back
you sink in
to sleep

I am lying as still as I can trying to still my sleeplessness
I feel the breathing wall of you that's why I married you I say

to die with
completely
contradictory
as always
as always
to live with
you say
though I thought you were asleep

I am the wind you are
the grass blown back the grass I am
the grass you are the wind blown back the wind

Believing

the task
>   given, chosen, granted
not from lack of belief in the thing

not even any more from lack of belief
>   it could be your task
not even so much any more that you can't do it
but that you *really* can't do it

get it into the world –
something to keep you from your own fear –

not so much like a young woman
>   who can't believe
>   what she can't see
>   even though her body assures her

>   something is happening
but that it could really go off on its own
and what then –

and if you could believe it, it would be like going back
even further
like putting all that turbulence of your thirties and forties
in perspective
putting all that erotic turbulence of your twenties aside and

making a promise based on nothing
but that promising,

>   believing
all this   you might make it

every day   for however long

Body of work

As coming upon
a puff-adder coiled on the carpet
under the desk

or a boomslang
slithered off out of its tracks
then its skin and later even
its bones...

perhaps they didn't even know it
was done when it was done,
those alchemists,

perhaps it felt too easy –
like waking drugged out of sleep still
sloughing it off –

maybe they didn't even feel better
for a while, if at all
after all

they didn't know what they were doing
when they started
nor how terrible they'd feel
nor for how long –

they were dead scared
was it the fear itself or was it the fear
of mercury poisoning or the poisoning itself

god's truth they must have got sick of it –
right arms aching down to the little finger
right side of the head aching
right down the back aching

sick of it sick of that vocation that exhaustion that compulsion
to make something of something as nothing
as love making matter what mattered
so little to anyone else if at all –

ridicule, poverty, social ostracism
they weren't worried about those they worried
about their work
not working their fear not resolving

what they knew: what they were
working on
their material, their metal, to make
come like the mysterious body

they didn't want to end up with
the same stuff they started with
the residue of the time before

all they knew they were
burning thickening melting
into air finding wanting
all they could ever hope for

Came back wanting

1

Silence   space   silver distance
clearly   for some   reason
     unknown
cold and the last night
cold to the bones
     of the Malutis

     shuddering in Ladybrand like panic

    from Aliwal North
rising beside us in the morning
     hundreds-of-million-years-old hills
     like cold blooded likkewaans.

2

Came back wanting
came home wanting to fill the gaps where I gave up
the embroidery for the cot –
what seems like a life ago
and the gaps growing

little figures with balloons alone in their cross stitch lines
pink cats and brown and black houses
strange tree, stick form candelabra holding the burning birds
blue and purple and red
stiff four fringed flowers –
angular, like the border for a fairy story
you can never return to –

cover all around with the covering of discrete leaves
cover the prince and horsemen,
cover the mounted prince and his footmen,
a frieze of real leaves:
jakalsbessie, umkhuhlu, compound, flowering, fruiting,
simple, silver, appleblaar, terminalia

and out of these:
glimpses of faces
side-striped jackal, african wild cat, rooikat, spotted serval
as he looks up suddenly
the face-on face of leopard
cheetah with the dark brown down
from his eyes down his mouth
like Michael's dark markings in the lines of a mouth drawn down
down his beard, down his chin –
don't even mention a lion –

3

Three years at least heading to this apotheosis
I want to say to my already grown children
I'm sorry, I'm sorry,
but for what?
God's ruthlessness?

Perhaps grief knows what, why
crying in front of the elephant
sluffing its slow trunk in front of the fence in front of us
in the river bed at Talamati,
crying and crying all the way from Nhlanguleni to where the road joins
to Skukuza
grief remembered somewhere
some spirit of tenacity glimpse of god-given lion-like inspiration.

4

Vehement and emphatic
or was it *emphatic and strident* the tone
I heard repeating itself
             like sickness
             like bile
"I have to *face* death" "to *answer* it" –

god knows
        what poison had driven me
             to such hubris

I'll tell you:
something terrible:
a woman could come home
and kill herself.

Eight years to the day but today I don't feel it
as my brother, Dave, *Duif,*
when he came home from the army,
on a morning like this walking along the river
"I know it's beautiful but I can't feel it".

Eight years since the day we took the canoes down the river
and her eldest son, my brother, Peter, took the photographs
incarnating forever
across the dark curve of the water
my son and my daughter, her grandson and granddaughter.
Incarnate, determined, confused, soft, Paul's and Frances's faces.

5

There are things that happen and they are only the beginnings
of hell – we think we know them –
and our children have to go out and live with them –
they are here – right in this valley –
a man murders his girlfriend's sister after he has raped her –
your niece is raped outside her flat in Rosebank and dragged off to Guguletu
and laughed at and abandoned –
another niece wakes weeping because she can't fit in to the right jeans
and all her friends will despise her –
your secretary's daughter is lying in a hospital in George
with the effects of other people's desires
cut more clearly by her own other hand into her own body –
in Rio, ten thousand "disappeared" by drug warlords;
in Zimbabwe in Afghanistan in Iraq
in *Bristol*
a hundred disaffected dragged a paramedic out of the ambulance and stoned it
after a young woman stabbed a man to death.

6

Dominic, young man, brave heart, *belonging to the Lord,*
Frances's travelling companion
and for that journey, ours,

in that wide bushveld warmth
on that Olifants bridge
above the rocks and reeds
        seeing through the clear water below
        terrapins swimming in ecstasy

(while everyone else was looking across and into the bush
 where the lion went in and we once saw a leopard
over *there*   disappear)

"*this* is ecstasy"

        and I didn't say what I didn't say
        I thought   I couldn't feel it;

what I felt
was exhausted

running from nothing
as if if I couldn't keep up it would kill me

what I felt, afterwards, anyway, thinking back
was exhausted, finished, exhausted –

I thought, now that there's nothing to do but stop
it could even
leave me alone.

7

Order – number –
count the years like the miles
not recorded the log book not kept –
turn them into a tapestry like a tree
flaked with brilliance,

scraps of life like faces
like Buonaguida's tree in the city of flowers
(in the Accademia, in Florence)
each gleaming incident hung along its branches
from a central spine, like the scales of a crocodile,

or leaves, a primitive book, an epic –

start with nought
two thousand and nought:
the annunciation: the three kings on the road outside Crocodile Bridge
two thousand and one:
the family hunting in the dark in the vlei next to the river
muscles bodies faces intent –
the dark, the hush, the grunts, the scent –
two thousand and two the two in the sun, twice,
two thousand and three – the Kalahari –

and so on – can a poem be a chronicle –
there are ways of writing a poem and reasons
but I forget them; the only one I know:
try – from your life – for some reason obscure –

tell me this is obvious and not good enough not enough
a poem being always eventually an act
of synchronicity –

     8
As it was the day
our dog, Henry, began his last
(his legs collapsed –
shit on the stoep
every morning for weeks
but this morning also vomit);

that morning Paul was drawing
for an art exam
he didn't know what
(he hadn't heard about Henry);

he had nothing planned nothing
but charcoal
lines settling through
erotic frustration,
imagination,
like damp eyelashes
of a sleeping child,
from an ellipse, and ovoid oasis
(the eagle of death or a road kill);

I walked with Frances when she refused finally
to write any more philosophy
having wrestled for days
love's wounds festering for months –

found stones on the slope on the Wild Side
laid out in single centres where the waves eroded
wings limbs flames;

all day next day
father, husband, Michael ached
having dug the bull of a grave
his king dog deserved.

9

Synchronicity
what seems like the first cliché you were taught about poems

meaning and matter coming together
the poet interpreter and dreamer
for instance

in the dark before dawn, in the car lights
like eight little fires bobbing over the dip
in the track at the crossroad
brighter, lighter and more persistent
once you've seen them there's no mistaking.

10

Suddenly the season changes and where you are
isn't *there* any more –
where you were wasn't *there* in the first place.

I can't keep everything in mind at once
I realise *where you are* means
where I am
I will never be
that poet, *that* person.

11

Poem; if I could find you, make you
cut the course
for the panic to come
into the warmth
rising

like the river rising in its saline bed
the poor fields salting,
earth worms drowning,
sacred ibis feasting,
planes cursed at their roots where the conservationists claim
they should never have been planted –
the guardians of the reserve will not open the mouth –
the river's malignant silence they can't hear
like they couldn't read the destruction last year
in the floods
they can't imagine
why you might spend your working life
(as does my other brother, Christopher,)
husbanding the fields
when *nature* grants a sinecure
to do nothing.

12

Look: look at your son, your daughter, look at their lives
in their faces, look into their faces
like in the lamplight when there's no electricity –

look, this isn't polemic, it's a poem
and the only way to make it
        from my life –
it can't be hurried, it can't be helped,
I can't think
my daughter will be home on Sunday and I haven't really begun –
I can't think
my son's exams will be over in two weeks and what then –
look, I can travel and travel looking
        for inspiration

but when it doesn't arise
think   it's only the cold side of creation
making you cry after your drive
you can say to yourself in exhaustion
it is only the malignant spirit
        of non existence
travels with me
like low lying mountains
for miles –

Twee Rivieren

Citrusdal, Clanwilliam, up over the Bokkeveld berge
into obliterating rain past Calvinia,
Brandvlei, stinking of cat piss, dog shit and mud
carried into the car as we got out of there –
thought there couldn't be a more depressing hotelier –
but past Verneukpan and on to the next proprietor
so lief vir die Here – we knew she wanted to save us
but from what – on our way anyway: transfrontier –
Kgalagadi, hot as Geelhoutvlei's boiler;

        where did it start
we asked ourselves a number of times
where it always starts, travelling, uncertainly
why here, in February,
     why feel compelled to do this:
     all those reasons
     not to want to

     I don't know
     but I do
     can I help it second guessing meaninglessness

50, 51, 52 in the shade the heat immeasurable, immense
bodies' effort that last night at Twee Rivieren so intense
the pushed-together beds rift like the Auob and Nossob

we laughed, and we laughed, and we laughed
and we laughed and laughed and laughed
LAUGHED n laughed n laughed n laughed;
laughlaughlaughlaughlaugh
and still it wasn't enough so we laughed and LAAAUGHED some more;

and now I remember some of the talk before,
two nights before,
two veins, I was crying,
weeping our various despairs

(and the first part of the Nossob closed
because of deep pools and sticky patches
after the rain the road turned in parts to almost river here
and there again
and then they opened it
so we didn't have to go up the Auob again
and across the dunes
after all);

two courses
        of anxiety and strength
family and work
and your family – which is mine – which made me cry again –
and your family – which is not mine – and your work –
and mine – trying to understand and crying again –

and our challenge at the confluence
words for the feeling for the thought for the confluence

the intensity of every night
every day each event every day's sight

on hot sand and on mud and in kameeldoring shade and in flight
yellow billed kite who isn't here any more
now you are black,
        black kite, black harrier,
black-chested, brown snake, immature bateleur,
booted, tawny, sandy, golden really,
kings of the birds, queens,
hunching, hiding, scanning, skimming really preying,

forgive me, I'm unsure, I'm sure
        I confuse you –

        that afternoon, at Nossob,
        chest on one bed heels on the other
        suspended   under the fan

        heat daze
        brick hot outside

I thought when you see me like this without any clothes
and call me beautiful really you are seeing yourself

or is it the other way round   51 in the shade

I close my eyes I realise
it's something as simple as this
if I don't see what you see I am shutting you off from yourself.

At Urikaruus we woke to continue our conflict
but this time in whispers so quiet
I can't recall what we said
except I said: don't wake me
but as I rolled over you were whispering wake up!
at the waterhole three lions and a cub
in the morning bronze and the breeze and
it seemed like only a moment but when we looked
it was possibly an hour
up   and into the dunes –

　　　　that was the morning after the afternoon before

　　　　I spread wet
　　　　towels over ourselves
　　　　I want to say
　　　　to make it easy

but deranged even in the aftermath
like *na-dors*, headache,
I can still speak only in grunts.

(Afterwards, after these travels,
I imagine when I wake
two poor people
riding their cart back
somewhere along the homeward track
outside Prieska, no shade, so they eat under their cart
and lie down on an old spread mat –
and that's when it starts

sometimes I see them doing it somewhere in the back
of an old station wagon
under the mountain fringes in the sun's rest at Beaufort West);

aftermath for days headache inertia
even when we come home

I could lie like that lion rolling onto the
almost falling into
the road,
smothered with butterflies
we wondered if he was sick –

I want to do it
but maybe I can't do the whole journey in one day
maybe that's just animus, possessed, hubris
maybe it's time to take myself for a walk –

always at the beginning and afterwards this questioning
like the travel itself the destination – why here, in February –

we asked ourselves
though I can't remember the words themselves

but you kept telling me:
already there, to come back   when I needed –
'you' are the other person
yr vr lvng hsbnd
in the text –

> (Jesus, why is this so slow –
> I'm so slow I can tell you I can't even speak –
> slow change perhaps that change
> of life
> keeps taking me
> ways I don't expect)

tender, skin of ground after rain, sore, tender in places
too many ecstatic animals like the two hartebeeste,
heart horns locked,
down on their knees,
penises erect,
thumping and butting
but butterflies butterflies over every muddy puddle

opened closed brushed
pushed pressed convulsed

at this conjunction

even when we are finished, dry,
dead   as two river beds.

Crossing the Crocodile

I can tell you: it wasn't something we could discuss too closely
to decide, to come here, to see you –
the cost, our debt, the distance, my daughter's tests and her thesis:

we got in my little car with our books and we drove like hell
two thousand five hundred kilometres if you count them from home
and on the way back four hours of *Purgatory* to listen to still.

A cobra, across the road as quick as thought a cobra, we think,
on the way here, it hadn't the fuse-like tubular intensity of a mamba –
on a rock, blinking in the heat, in the north wind: freckled nightjar;

but even here, to *write* – we think
that's why we came here –
so, strange, naturally, it's not really easy,

*"they will look round for poetry, and will be induced to inquire by what species
of courtesy these attempts can be permitted to assume that title"*
so I note simply: Appelblaar in flower;

the doctor said: make something frivolous, do something frivolous –
though I know whatever I write is frivolous, useless, law unto itself,
isn't it depressing, like my life: utterly frivolous, but still, to be happy!

> *Hymn to the sickle-bush and appelblaar in flower*
> I would write you, if I felt the need, sing
> sickle-bush what you need: you need nothing:
>
> suspending beside the hide above the river
> your pendulous purple sterile splendour
> tipped with its fertile feathery yellow flower
>
> what you need –
> not songs, names,
> you are named: dichrostachys cinerea
>
> no, no doubt
> you need your name
> no doubt it tells us

what we don't know
how you grow
how much water you need, who you feed

but a *song* like that collared sunbird sings,
(and even the bird-books can't get it truer
"a high pitched chirri chirri chirri")

sweet sickle bush, over the Crocodile river
(where it sings over its stones,
Crocodile, Ngwenya),

who will love you if we don't,
no doubt you don't grow for our happiness
but can't I share it with you there in your thicket?

You know, I know there've been songs: who provides
wood for whom, wooden songs, what firewood, who takes
what wood to make fire, what fire, to feed whom?

But sickle bush, waving above the early morning river,
(and just across the bank on the other side: leafless acacia,
surreal sticks sticking up out of nothing)

it's as silly and simple as
can be
to be happy. It's my need.

Appelblaar – whom my mother used always to call,
formally, your proper name,
lonchocarpus capassa –

here you are, suddenly, arms full:
mauve, delicate lilac, even paler purple –
like the mother of the bride, mother of all brides,

mother of the mother of the bride –
who knows how long, appelblaar,
your brief: flower: November,

one tree, one at a time, on the dry banks of the Bume, only?
Always all I've seen before is your strangely
lovely, simple-leafy, greeny-grey motley.

Sickle bush, appleblaar, freckled nightjar,
I'll tell you something sweet – you live close to hell,
and you know as well that other fenced off place, mythical…

yours, ours, those lions on the bank
while the light so complete in descent the white
on the undersides and legs:

trunks: logs: sticks
it's this
metamorphosis.

✦

Ancient Jakalsbessie –
what's such urgency
you wake me at three

huge and gentle in the grey wind
moving, unmoving,
waking with pale little flowers, don't they sleep,

do they open and open insistently, inconspicuously,
there next to the kigelia tree,
skinny baboons stripping the pods, skinning the sausages, green,

the flower on the jakalsbessie waits, the bush waits,
the male and female flowers
on the ancient jakalsbessie wait in their pale restraint;

the Crocodile waits for no-one
ruthless it follows its happiness over the stones
it survives.

✦

Aristotle, my daughter tells me, said
civilisation begins when we're no longer at the mercy
of the elements;

" Aristotle, I have been told.." (at my daughter's age,
it was Wordsworth who told me)
"… Poetry is the most philosophic of all writing…truth with its own testimony."

Bitterness.
No hope.
That's why they died.

Reflection: consciousness conscious of itself.
This bushveld, this lowveld, these banks of this Crocodile –
sacred fringes of the pools of ourselves

sacred space of reflection
if you show me myself
how   I am! Even in drought!

We will not fall into ourselves into our own reflections
too little time! we are given
too close to the border the highway close by:

Mozambique, illegal immigrants, fields filled with shacks, Ngwavuma,
with people with AIDS, malaria, Komati under its flaming flamboyants,
children squatting in the early sun, waiting for the bus, for school.

And on the hot sandy flanks of Ngwenya
two dead impala:
was it bitterness, tannin, self-protection, trees in drought?

But today, see who I saw today:
combreta, combreta, combreta
coming into life again

bushwillows, coming after
your four winged pods
sweetness of spikelets!

and the engine switched off at the reservoir, surprised:
"silently and very fast", the elephants crossing,
the mother as if she could pick up, carry

73

the shambling still hairy calf, tender, with her trunk,
then that phalanx of trunks,
drinking, determined, efficient, fast –

✦

Yesterday we were discussing
reflection and projection, my daughter and I,
on a long stretch, dry,

nothing
but leafless acacia standing
like burnt sticks, thickets of misunderstanding –

today as we stop to look up against the light
at that morning martial eagle
she signals the thrill with the urgent tap:

it is dawn, it is grey, it has stormed in the night,
through the dormant sticks,
a hint of damp:

the civet:
spottier, blacker, bigger
than we could ever

have imagined had we imagined
we might ever see him at all:
he takes no notice, he is nosing after his own pursuits,

nose to the earth, to whatever it delivers, the damp earth,
he delivers us from ourselves, takes us way out beyond
the anthills and stumps of our own reflections

way out of time, control, speech, all we see is
this:
once in a lifetime life!

Bush, sweet bush, ruthless dry bush, sweet at last
with pale stipples of stamens and stipules,
and that black-blotched hyena-high civet!

We are alone, this mother I am, this daughter,
we follow him on, after, on and way out
of our own thoughts, with the sound of barbet, cicada,

I can't even remember, the scent of combreta,
and on, on this high bank, this dry river,
the twelve – in the shade – pride of the pride.

✦

Sacred space, how do I thank you!
How few of us there have been, how few and how few
generations and how little time left!

There is a photo of my grandfather
bending over an open fire beside a mud hut at Letaba
in white shirt and black tie.

This is my grandfather, the perfect marksman, the big shot,
QC, conservationist, communist, listed, atheist,
this is the one whose elders were shocked:

even as a youngster: published a paper:
the importance   of miscegenation.
miscegenation, like *sex across the colour bar*

like some prurient school-boy punishment
like *kissing the rod* – and god knows what
you do about love perhaps or happiness –

see, we come from this species
of women, my daughter and I, who care so bitterly
they kill themselves over it! Look, I know how lucky I am

to survive this bitterness so far bring myself here.
It's only History destines me to insignificance, irrelevance, frivolousness!
For God's sake, can't I give myself this!

✦

Boys left at home, husband, son, perhaps son-in-law to be,
I give you back – your generosity, letting us come, helping us be
without envy, jealousy, where you would also love to be –

75

boys, what you didn't see:
one large leopard lay along the length of a broad-pod albizia tree;
a weir of stones and still some of the Sabi whispering, singing;

have you ever heard a lioness pant – here,
so close, you can hear
the tongue slap-slap in her throat

let alone the rasp against
rufus pink along the legs
she now   and then   lick-licks

you may think she is alone
but as you turn there are three others
throwing their arms around her, literally –

and at last the krag-mannetjie
in all his maan-haar
fiery sexual energy.

✦

At night, it is not this intensity
comes to torment me:
miserable self-pity;

> I am alone, lady, and lost as
> the daughter I cannot find
> the child I agreed to give a lift to.

> Lady, like any other
> rich kids' boarding school mother –
> only, everyone else has everything

> under control on their cell phones
> and only I
> am left in a panic

> in my sister-in-law's dressing gown
> and lipstick.
> And I can't find the child let alone the mother.

Meanwhile the table fills: everyone coming to the party;
and I have to get up and go,
dressing gown disguised under a blanket –

women in your high shoes
and smooth skins
my own

deep misanthropy, misogyny,
you shame me;
but still, still I still want to be one of you, part of the party!

Shoppers, pleasure seekers, readers
of novels everyone is talking about
in the Sunday papers

and everyone thinks anyone could write
if only they had the time
and quite probably they might.

Why do you come here
to shame me
my shape, my shame, my envy?

I wake with the ache of loneliness
but here comes my daughter bringing me tea!
And back to her ethics thesis.

What more could I want?
The night to bring me Khulile,
like at the start of the journey,

I woke the poet before I left home,
Khulile, the poet, Khulile, kissing me,
waking that dream, that energy right through me –

here I have dreamt my in-laws: dreamt they despise me;
and, intensely, test anxiety, for me
for some inexplicable reason, and for my daughter accompanying me;

this morning, this clattering, hot wind blowing,
and we're faced away from the river
so you'd think we'd concentrate better;

what do I want: to wake that need, again, fulfilling it, through me
I want Lesego and Angifi and Vonani
and Robert's tender arms assuring me,

I want them not to laugh and say
"in your dreams, lady";
even more shamelessly: I want them to love me.

Why did we come here, my daughter and I?
writing, speaking, listening, being
together; spoken about wedding dresses and happiness,

human flourishing, and is it eschatology or teleology –
we have listened to Dante's *Purgatory* –
her gift to me –

each has written, and she has read to me
and I am still ashamed, reader, listener,
I have responded like this old fashioned mother

with all that free floating anxiety, I have given her *advice*
as bad as "don't forget your seat belt" "hide your passport"
"have you taken your malaria *muti*?"

✦

Once I wrote in a transport of delight
but no-one knew what to make of it,
no-one wanted anything to do with it.

Work like anyone's work only
also transport, play; work like any
work to take you across the great water.

> *"What country, friends, is this..."*
> *"And what should I do"* across the Ngwenya
> *"my brother he is in Elysium"*

78

What do I want across the Ngwenya, where despite the relief
of the rain, the haak-en-steek's gradual re-leaf (or is it all imaginary)
I still want the wildness of wild dog I have never seen

the ordinary doggedness of wild dog.
Cross the Crocodile.
Across the river:

the heat, the infinite, infinitesimal, intimate scents
babbles and whispers of birds and mammals
and shh shhh shhhs of sands and winds

and whistles, incessant alarms, trickles of trees
like the shimmy of a shudder
squirrel   sap itself.

✦

This morning –
only his arousing
grunting, groaning, in the bush

I Am Here I Am Here I Am Here
so deep in the thicket
we can't see him –

last evening, at first through the grass
the pale part of a belly,
at first, that's all we could see –

and the Englishman drove past him,
though we pointed him out, he doubted:
"would he stand up in a court of law" –

God! How he'd have laughed on the other side of his face
when they stood up and were counted!
the three kings, I could say, and feasting

so close we could hear the determined tearing, swallowing
in the falling dark we could hardly tear ourselves away
two minutes late at the gate and worth every minute rule breaking.

But this morning nothing but reminding –
the guttural uh uh uh, uh uh uh
here, I am here, I am here.

✦

She has read to me from the book of philosophy
 I gave her for her twenty first birthday;
"it's here, isn't it, here, this, where we are":

"...and, finally, the eschatological May-be
unfolds not just as can-be
but as should-be –

in short, less a power of immanent potency
driving toward fulfilment
than as a power of the powerless

which bids us remain open to the possible divinity
whose gratuitous coming – already, now, and not yet –
is always a surprise and never without grace."

✦

From where I am alone in the hide:
across the river bed
two impala: dead;

six kudu bulls crossing
six kudu bulls through the reeds and the rocks
huge horns twisting, disappearing, reappearing, leaping the crossing;

through my mind, from nowhere,
with this wind slight and this sight from the hide,
my own words, from six months past:

> you love me in despair
> who can ask for more
> whatever it means, to love me in despair,
>
> it means what I cannot say
> more simply, you love me in despair
> what does it mean;

no-one else on earth;
what are the words, love, despair,
stones, weights, weights on the diaphragm;

they mean: seen myself in my despair
not being able to cross I shall cross;
when I thought I was there I wasn't yet there;

✦

In the heat of the mid day
we are reminded again and again my god!
in the scant shade of the stunted terminalia

against the termite hill,
the sand coloured grass,
gracious, given, his presence.

To cross into his territory –
being, immanent, arriving,
reminding, being, be,

asleep, awake, alert, too hot to sleep,
afraid, intolerant, irritated,
(I must go to Komati to fix that tyre) but

like that likkewaan in the muddy pond, or the livid lizard, in wait for me,
where the thick billed weaver, white dot on his deep brown face
flashes: he is ready for a mate, threads through the reeds

his intricacy, extreme delicacy, not as hardy
as the hanging baskets of his spectacled or masked neighbours,
this feeling as fragile and carried away in the storm, perhaps, but happy.

I go down to the hide, write one line, one word;
she sits at her computer and the rhythmic ticks
give her away: it's just a game.

Every day we make the crossing:
this territory with its smudge of sights and smells
and some incredibly, vividly, indelibly –

but at night, like the book club ladies
who sat in their circle and judged me,
and now come up in the supermarket practically

kissing me, gingerly approaching me, reproaching me
phantasms of anxiety cling to me –
who will guide me through this purgatory?

Only leaves to trees,
animals, insects, reptiles, birds,
my daughter's passionate faith-filled philosophy;

(and what this means is uncertainty
she is preparing her leaving;
next year she'll be where? America?)

✦

Deep in the thick of mid-break mid-week mid-day heat
I have let go and slept –
twice I have slept for an hour each time –

now we are back on the fringes of the week,
of washing and fussing, of packing and return.
I lie like that lion too close to the road

even though my eyes close now and then
even though I shove deeper under the pillow
as he did into the ant-heap into the shade blinking, not sleeping:

vigilance; vigilant though the heat of the bush sings
it will go on just the same though the night frogs sing;
alert and sweaty, get up to shower before light – three;

I have been hijacked. I have lost my son,
my passport, cell-phone, ID, keys, money.
At last one of the four who hijacked me

lends me a phone – I phone the police –
the police come – they lend me a phone –
I phone my husband – he says "sorry".

What did I hope for? Hopelessly I hoped
for something transforming, letting
hopelessly, contradictorily, be, I hoped

to bring something back – way to be –
(frankly, simply, I wanted to sleep
and to learn how to sleep again without chemicals helping me,

and to come home again and be able to sleep, I wanted normality
to come home and feel normal, I can tell you, I know now this is
impossible, normality, normally, I don't even know what to think.)

How do we make it
this "may be" this maybe
we wait, when we can't find it or keep it

wait when we wake having lost it –
we swim, we feel the heat seep, we wish, we talk, we drive
and we drive and we look and smell and listen, write, dream and we sleep.

✦

Boys, is this boring, you know how it is, it is, sometimes, and the length
of the journey that makes it.
I'm sorry, it's boring, but believe me, looking back, there isn't a bit

you don't want
to go over; and over; the process of it, you go over and over
each sight each day recounting it, processing it;

you know how it is, you've been there and this time
you haven't and I can't
promise you anything but my fidelity:

I want more of this journey, I want for some undercurrent feeling
to tell it again and I don't know again I don't know how to begin again:
shadow, undertow, wake with this: wanting to go

back there: be there:
and even if I could, if I were to, would I come upon it again
like thirty two lions all counted or one

once in a life time civet
like any other epiphany or would I really recognise it:
this time – see it?

(And this is what happens on this kind of journey,
we go on too long, we get hungry, thirsty, we need to stop and to wee,
but sometimes, like not the second day or the third, all of it, we have it!)

✦

There is still the end of the journey:
Colesberg: ten to four, and I wake in exhaustion as I did the day before –
the dream forces the tears, through my closed lids, seeping

horrible as Dante through the theatre-voiced CD speaking
with that plum-in-his-mouth centuries-later-interpreter
of eyelids sewn through with lead! shut everlastingly!

God, Dante! What torture you dream up!
What false humility, pride disguised as pity!
 Give us Ovid any day, give us Milton,

Paradise Lost, rather than this, give us Dylan's
Desolation Row: that's what we play waiting at the stop/ry/go –
then, we *will not go down into the ground* –

and is it only defiance I dream of
to hurt me – I simply refuse
the man who waits for me – crying, use

this childish exasperation, exasperating strategy –
I *cannot*. No no no no no. I'm *married* can't you see!
He plays, he sings, I cry through closed lids, he wants me, waits for me.

✦

Four in the morning leafing through notebooks
largely illegible tracks back to
doubt, old stuff, dust, drought –

cold crocodile:
wanting energy, wanting drive, meat
thinking we were crossing

every day repeating was it only rehearsing
and now again retracing every day only
chronicle, do I only repeat?

Repeat, like a liar or a poet, as Deleuze says Hume says,
and I'm sure Shakespeare said it before them,
to make myself   believe.

Crocodile Chronicle:
though the number of ways seems limitless
really there is only one:

day by day, night by night, sight by smell by feel by taste by sight
crossing the same temporary crossing
the water running through the new road's drains –

third last day of our stay,
standing at the Kwikfit at Komati
swallows and swifts above and beyond

and under the old railway bridge, turning towards their paths of flight,
(and the swallows fly like this – shlff shlfff shlffff, so swiftly
but the swifts – god knows where they ever rest –

they only fly further
into this morning seven o clock grey morning light)
suddenly I see it, here, in the workshop in Komati,

every day, we are being dipped in the mystery –
daily how we are dipped remains the mystery –
"everything is a question of degree of belief even the delirium of non-knowledge"

don't let me go back there:
(before I left home, before that rhythm of crossing
repeating and repeating, each day's material being):

> **The wretched**
> *fear of hard work*
> *fear of will*

fear of self
fear of not knowing
fear of finding nothing but

fear of my own fear
no guide, no law, no actuality,
no authority:

that sober judge this, that drunken one that;
this president, that –
and the ones who sang their praises, the women, the dresses, the hats –

fear of loneliness, uselessness, worthlessness, neglect, regret –
the sound of my own voice singing
my own thoughts

my own work
fear of this
fear of my own

death –
what I inherit –
all of this –

✦

I say to myself can't I just let it be –
what is was – let the chronicle rest, the chronicler rest
chronic restlessness, unrest –

if I don't make something of it, it won't let me rest, if I don't
make some song more satisfactory, (chirri chirri chirri)
it will always be less, if I don't continue to chuck away all the unnecessary

notes, notebooks of notes,
give it its own space, unless
it feels its own breathing space

it will always be less
less – what it is, is less, what it was, is less –
less than it could be, maybe

that process of immanence,
presence,
that setting free –

so four in the morning to continue this travel
as it was in Colesberg, and for a fortnight before,
5 a.m, 4, 3.45, seemed impossible at first, then I gave in.

> This morning, no more than five faded roses
> after the long night's race –
> and the other woman has won something useful!

> A camera! and extending lens and all the time
> I thought we were on the same team!
> I don't want your wrapped roses: pitiful!

Start again then, nearly at the end:
something happened at Komati
in that muddy lot of the tyre shop;

something I happened *to see*; to do with daily mystery.
Flat topped low hanging flamboyant trees,
children waiting for school beside the sugar cane fields,

a man baptising my tyre in his water trough out at the back
while I quickly noted the swallows…
(it lasted just long enough: a bit flat in Colesberg

and in Cape Town the rasta man in Observatory
telling me how worn they were
selling me two new tyres – just didn't see….)

Komati: and the tyres took us to cross the Crocodile
the rain beginning in sheets, sluicing
every game path, every plane a lake, every mud hole a whole dam

every runnel in the road, every dip, we wondered
if we'd get through, like a river itself, pouring with the pressure
of months and months and months of no water at all.

And suddenly a plain full of flowers through the rain
where yesterday bare earth today: these, already beginning to bedraggle,
white star shaped flowers, I don't even know what they are;

we forgot to ask anyone,
by the time we saw anyone they were already so far
un-named, opened, star white, sickle thin, close to the ground

our last gift, before the bush itself greening, and steaming,
the koppies gleaming, in
"perfectly useless concentration"

two males are given to us –
alone –
walking towards us, sniffing their territory, marking their ways –

they are our last gift
their ochre eyes through ours:
into the inner retinas.

✦

I lost the thread of this chronicle:
scraps notes, impressions, repetitions;
    dream-like, like that image of my old father standing

      under some generic tree – mother of all trees –
      reminding me, like at the head of the table the patriarch
      reminds me, I didn't get the job as a singer –

I've lost the dream of the old poet teacher
who beats the long lines' rhythms
with a stick who reads (breath) and reads my lines (breath)

and as he reads
the lions look up
from the long grass (breathe)

he reads in the beat-beat
as they at the crossroads
head up –

he reads the long discursive lines
like through long grass
as if they were real –

no question
of competition, of the better version:
but his words, measure, solemn, beat, I have lost them!

Lost the rhythm of the road where we followed the animal rhythms,
rhythms of the storm and sun and wind;
hands like a baboon's, dropped, open,

the lion's eyes, boring through me in all my twittering inconsequentiality,
lost the civet's nose,
the steenbuck's and hare's ears, their veined sensitivity,

tongues of giraffe, trunks of elephant and tree –
and the river, and the river crossing, gone, done,
crossed into that reality –

Notes and Acknowledgements

As the ancient alchemists intuited, and as depth psychology recognises, all work is both work (in or on) material – the 'material world' – as well as work upon the individual psyche. The work of artists is close to play, and poets, who play with words, work on, or with, psyche's language. What the soul has to say is often out of tune with its time and place. At such times and places, other poets, alive or dead, are the ones who bring comfort and inspiration. Throughout this book I quote or refer to poets (as well as some psychologists and philosophers) whose work has made mine possible.

Points on poems

William Carlos Williams, "no ideas but in things"; *Paterson*

John Keats, "happy, happy"; *Ode on a Grecian Urn*

Angifi Dladla, "the energy that's divine"; *Song of the fertility doll*

T.S.Eliot, "the still point of the turning world"; *Little Gidding*

William Shakespeare, "sixth and lastly"; Dogberry the constable in *Much Ado About Nothing*

Louise Glück "not the apotheosis but the pattern"; *Ripe Peach*

Gilles Deleuze on Nietzsche "affirmation of the affirmation"; *Pure Immanence*

Robert Duncan, Scales of the Marvelous; the title to a book on his work subtitled *working papers in contemporary criticism.*

James Hillman "The activity of perception or sensation in Greek is aesthesis which means at root 'taking in' and 'breathing in' – a 'gasp', that primary aesthetic response"; *The heart's thought*

Penelope

Ruth Miller, "The pure necessity – a shroud"; *Spider*

I Ching, "the hard and strong", Hexagram 41, Diminution.

Anne Sexton, as an epigraph to her *Selected Poems* quotes Kafka: "the books we need are the kind that act upon us like a misfortune, that make us suffer like the death of someone we love more than ourselves, that make us feel as though we were on the verge of suicide…a book should serve as the axe for the frozen sea within us."

Her letters, referred to in this poem, are edited by her daughter Linda Gray Sexton and Lois Aimes *Anne Sexton, a self-portrait in letters*, first published in 1977 shortly after her suicide.

Luke, 12.48 *The Bible*, "Of those to whom much is given, much will be required"

Euripides, "O my father, had I the tongue of Orpheus to make the stones to leap and follow me…do not take away this life of mine before its dying time" – at the age of 13 I performed the role of Iphigenia in a school production of *Iphigenia in Aulis*: I have no record of whose translation we used.

Alan Finlay, "I fish in your give"; *wind and sea*

Alchemical Incantations

The epigraph to "Alchemical Incantations" is taken from the introduction, p4 and p14, to Edward Edinger's "Anatomy of the Psyche"; (Open Court 1994)

Burnt Offering

Elizabeth Bishop, "How – I didn't know any word for it – how 'unlikely'"; *In the Waiting Room*

Lesego refers to the poet Lesego Rampolokeng

Virginia Woolf creates a character, Lily Briscoe, an artist, in *To the Lighthouse*

Down to Earth

Richard Murphy was married to the poet and novelist Patricia Avis.

Incarnate

Denise Levertov, *Conversation in Moscow*

Rock

The Scorpions, "rock you like a hurricane"

Deep Purple, "smoke on the water, fire in the sky"

Bury the Dead

Terence Rattigan who wrote the play *Who is Sylvia?*, the poet Sylvia Plath, her friend and critic Al Alvarez, the actress Gwyneth Paltrow, the film *Sylvia,* are all referred to in the first section;

Mphutlane wa Bofelo, "kill the poet" "kill the white woman"; *poem circulated by email*

Louise Bogan, "Henceforth, from the mind,/For your whole joy, must spring"; *Henceforth From the Mind*

William Carlos Williams, "It is all according to the imagination", "being a poet/ could have given them" "to partake of the host/ laid for them and for me"; *The Host*

Come together

Hexagram 32 of *I Ching* "the institution of marriage...the enduring union...soft and compliant inside"

Came back wanting

This poem recalls trips from our home above the Goukamma River in the Southern Cape to the Kruger National Park; many specific places, flowers, trees and animals found there are named.

"Buonaguida's tree", however, refers to the painting in the Galleria dell'Accademia, in Florence, painted at the turn of the fourteenth century by Pacino di Buonaguida called "Tree of Life".

Twee Rivieren

Twee Rivieren is the name of the main camp in the Kgalagadi Transfrontier Park; the camp is close to the confluence of the Auob and Nossob rivers along whose beds or banks the two main roads run. The second largest camp in the park is Nossob.

Crossing the Crocodile

William Wordsworth, "they will look around for poetry, and will be induced to inquire by what species of courtesy these attempts can be permitted to assume that title" "Aristotle, I have been told...Poetry is the most philosophic of all writing...truth with its own testimony"; *Preface to the Lyrical Ballads*

W. H. Auden, "silently and very fast"; *The Fall of Rome*

"Khulile", "Lesego", "Angifi", "Vonani", "Robert" refer to the poets Khulile Nxumalo, Lesego Rampolokeng, Angifi Dladla, Vonani Bila and Robert Berold.

Shakespeare, *Twelfth Night*, Viola, "What country, friends, is this?" "And what should I do [in Illyria]? My brother, he is in Elysium"

Richard Kearney, "And, finally, the eschatological May-be unfolds not just as can-be ... but as should-be...in short, less as a power of immanent potency driving toward fulfillment than as a power of the powerless which bids us remain open to the possible divinity whose gratuitous coming – already, now, and not yet – is always a surprise and never without grace". *The God Who May Be*, Indiana University Press, 2001.

Bob Dylan "[we] will not go down into the ground"; *Let me die in my footsteps*

Gilles Deleuze "everything is a question of degree of belief even the delirium of non-knowledge" *Pure Immanence*, Zone Books, New York, 2005;

Elizabeth Bishop, "perfectly useless concentration". Letter to Anne Stevenson.

Other poetry titles by Modjaji Books

Fourth Child
by Megan Hall

Life in Translation
by Azila Talit Reisenberger

Please, Take Photographs
by Sindiwe Magona

Oleander
by Fiona Zerbst

Strange Fruit
by Helen Moffett

Invisible Earthquake
A Women's Journal Through Stillbirth
(Poetic Memoir)
by Malika Ndlovu

http://modjaji.book.co.za